1000

Tricky Word Problems

For Class- 3 & 4

(For Math Olympiad and Practice)

By

Dr.Antarjeeta Nayak

PREFACE

In the vibrant world of mathematics, word problems are more than just exercises—they are bridges connecting mathematical concepts to real-world experiences. This collection of challenging and engaging word problems has been carefully curated to inspire young minds and build critical skills that extend beyond the classroom. Each problem is a puzzle waiting to be solved, encouraging children to apply logic, reasoning, and creativity to a variety of practical scenarios.

Through word problems, children learn that mathematics is not merely a collection of abstract numbers and symbols but a toolkit that helps us understand, interpret, and solve everyday challenges. These problems range across fundamental topics such as money management, distance measurement, geometry, time, calendar calculations, patterns, and fractions. Each question is designed to simulate real-life situations, requiring children to interpret scenarios, make calculations, and track values carefully—skills essential for problem-solving in any field.

In exploring money problems, children practice budgeting, saving, and making purchasing decisions, while geometry problems lead them to think spatially, using area, perimeter, and symmetry to solve visual puzzles. Tally mark and calendar problems bring structure and sequence to their mathematical thinking, reinforcing their understanding of counting, organization, and date-based calculations. Time-focused problems teach practical skills in managing hours and minutes, helping children appreciate the value of time while mastering conversions, addition, subtraction, multiplication, and division. The variety of patterns, reasoning puzzles, and mental arithmetic challenges in this collection encourage students to recognize trends and build quick calculation skills. These carefully designed exercises foster logical reasoning, strategic thinking, and an ability to analyse and solve problems creatively.

By engaging with these word problems, children will not only develop confidence in handling diverse mathematical scenarios but also experience the joy of discovery and mastery in math. This journey into real-life applications, clever puzzles, and complex reasoning problems will prepare children for advanced problem-solving, empowering them with skills that last a lifetime.

Dive into this adventure and watch as the world of math comes alive, revealing its power, beauty, and endless possibilities!

1.	Write the place value of the digit 5 in 5,678.
2.	What is the expanded form of 3,209?
3.	Write 7,504 in words.
4.	What is the number that comes after 6,899?
5.	Write the smallest 4-digit number.
6.	Write the largest 3-digit number.
7.	Round 3,497 to the nearest hundred.
8.	What is the sum of the digits in 4,321?
9.	What is the difference between the place values of 7 in 7,125 and 5,170?
10.	Write the number that comes before 2,001.
11.	Convert the Roman numeral XIV to a Hindu-Arabic number.
12.	What is the Roman numeral for 38?
13.	Convert XL to a Hindu-Arabic number.
14.	Write the Roman numeral for 75.
15.	What is XXVII in Hindu-Arabic numerals?
16.	Convert 53 to Roman numerals.
17.	What is the Roman numeral for 99?

18.	Convert the Roman numeral LXXII to a Hindu-Arabic number.
19.	Write 85 as a Roman numeral.
20.	Convert XC to Hindu-Arabic numerals.
21.	Add 2,345 and 4,678.
22.	Subtract 5,629 from 7,890.
23.	If you add 3,456 and 2,200, what is the result?
24.	Find the sum of 2,345, 1,234, and 3,456.
25.	Subtract 1,234 from 5,432.
26.	How much is 4,768 minus 3,123?
27.	A number is 2,345. If you subtract 1,000 from it, what will you get?
28.	Add 3,210 and 2,005.
29.	What is 9,999 minus 2,678?
30.	Find the difference between 4,567 and 3,123.
31.	Which is greater: XLIV or XXXIX?
32.	Compare LXXX and LXV using greater than (>), less than (<), or equal to (=).
33.	What is the next Roman numeral after XLVIII?

34.	Write the missing Roman numeral: LIV, LV, LVI, ___.
35.	Is LXVII greater than LXIV? (Yes or No)
36.	Multiply 23 by 4.
37.	Divide 640 by 8.
38.	If you multiply 45 by 5, what is the result?
39.	Divide 720 by 9.
40.	Multiply 56 by 10.
41.	If you divide 900 by 5, what do you get?
42.	What is 36 times 7?
43.	Divide 144 by 12.
44.	Multiply 15 by 8.
45.	What is the quotient when 450 is divided by 9?
46.	Add XV and XX. What is the result in Roman numerals?
47.	Subtract XII from XXV. What is the result in Roman numerals?
48.	Add L and XX. What is the result in Hindu-Arabic numerals?

49.	Subtract IX from XXI. Write the result in Hindu-Arabic numerals.
50.	If you add XXX and XV, what is the result in Roman numerals?
51.	What is the next number in the pattern: 101, 102, 103, ___?
52.	Compare 3,456 and 3,654 using greater than (>), less than (<), or equal to (=).
53.	Write all the even numbers between 10 and 20.
54.	What is the smallest number between 600 and 700?
55.	Write the next two numbers in the sequence: 150, 200, 250, ___, ___.
56.	Find the missing number: 900, 850, 800, ___, ___.
57.	Is 12 an odd or even number?
58.	Compare 7,321 and 7,123.
59.	Find the next number in the pattern: 10, 20, 30, ___.
60.	Which is greater: 4,321 or 4,231?

61.	Rina has 1,234 marbles. Her friend gave her 456 more. How many marbles does she have now?
62.	There are 7,892 books in a library. If 1,234 books are borrowed, how many are left in the library?
63.	A bus can carry 50 passengers. If 6 buses are full, how many passengers are there in total?
64.	A box contains 5,432 candies. If 1,234 candies are eaten, how many are left?
65.	Arjun read 234 pages of a book on Monday and 432 pages on Tuesday. How many pages did he read in total?
66.	There are 678 students in a school. If 123 students are absent, how many students are present?
67.	If a pack of pencils costs ₹25, how much do 8 packs cost?
68.	A shop has 1,000 apples. If 345 apples are sold, how many are left?
69.	Ria has 2,345 points in a game. If she earns 456 more, how many points does she have now?

70.	If there are 432 candies in one bag, how many candies are there in 5 bags?
71.	Rita wrote the number 4,508. She says the place value of 5 is fifty. Is she correct? Why or why not?
72.	The number 6,789 is written on the board. What will the number become if you replace the digit in the hundreds place with 4?
73.	John added 1,200 and 2,300. His answer was 3,500. Is he correct? If not, what mistake might he have made?
74.	Swap the digits in the tens and hundreds place of 5,372. What is the new number?
75.	Which is larger: The sum of the digits in 4,567 or the sum of the digits in 5,678?
76.	Find the next number in the pattern: 10, 20, 30, 40, ___? Explain your reasoning.
77.	What is the pattern in the sequence: 5, 10, 20, 40, ___? What will be the next number?
78.	You have a number that increases by 5 each time: 12, 17, 22, 27, ___. What is the next number?

79.	In a sequence: 1, 2, 4, 8, 16, _____, each number is twice the previous one. What will be the next two numbers?
80.	If a number pattern starts at 100 and decreases by 10 each time (100, 90, 80, ...), what will be the 6th number?
81.	Ravi has 345 apples, and he gave away 129. How many apples does he have now?
82.	If you subtract 432 from 987, will the answer be greater or smaller than 600?
83.	*If you subtract 5,432 from 9,999, will the result be larger than 4,500?*
84.	What is the product of 25 and 4?
85.	Divide 560 by 8. Will the quotient be larger or smaller than 80?
86.	Is 6 times 9 greater than 50?
87.	If you multiply 15 by 7, will the result be more or less than 100?
88.	A teacher has 36 pencils and wants to divide them equally among 9 students. How many pencils will each student get?
89.	Which is larger: 2,345 or 2,354? Explain how you can tell without subtracting.

90.	Is 5,678 smaller than 6,543? How do you know?
91.	Compare the numbers 9,012 and 8,999. Which is greater, and how did you decide?
92.	Arrange the following numbers in ascending order: 4,321, 3,210, 5,123.
93.	Which number is greater: the sum of 1,234 and 567, or the product of 123 and 4?
94.	If you add X and XV, what will the result be in Roman numerals? Show your working.
95.	Compare XL and XXXV. Which is larger? How did you determine that?
96.	What is the difference between XXIX and XV in Roman numerals?
97.	Is LX greater than LIV? Explain your reasoning.
98.	Find the next Roman numeral in the pattern: X, XX, XXX, ____. What is the rule of the pattern?
99.	What is the next Roman numeral after XXXVIII? How did you figure it out?
100.	Write the missing numeral in the sequence: XXIV, XXV, XXVI, ____?

101.	In a pattern of Roman numerals decreasing by 5 (XL, XXXV, XXX, ...), what will be the next two numerals?
102.	If you count in steps of 10 using Roman numerals starting from X, what will be the 5th number in the sequence?
103.	Add the Roman numerals XX and VIII. What is the sum in Roman numerals?
104.	Subtract XIV from XXV. What is the result in Roman numerals?
105.	If you add XIII and XVII, what will the result be in Hindu-Arabic numerals?
106.	What will be the difference when you subtract IX from XXIV in Roman numerals?
107.	Add XL and XV. What is the sum in Roman numerals?
108.	Ravi has XIII pencils. His friend gives him IX more pencils. How many pencils does Ravi have in total, in Roman numerals?
109.	A clock shows the time VIII. If 2 hours pass, what will the time be in Roman numerals?

110.	Sara needs to read XXV pages. She has already read XIV pages. How many more pages does she need to read?
111.	There are XXX students in a class. If VIII students leave the class, how many students are left in Roman numerals?
112.	A baker made XL cakes. He sold XII cakes. How many cakes does he have left, in Roman numerals?
113.	A factory produced 18,435 toys in January and 15,689 in February. How many toys did it produce in both months combined?
114.	A bookstore had 45,670 books. It sold 12,345 books and bought 8,765 new books. How many books does it have now?
115.	A city's population was 87,234 last year. This year, it increased by 12,567. What is the new population?
116.	A warehouse stored 24,568 boxes. 5,678 boxes were delivered, and 13,450 more boxes were added. How many boxes are in the warehouse now?
117.	A company made a profit of ₹76,532 in January, ₹42,689 in February, but lost ₹18,743

	in March. What was the total profit for these three months?
118.	A school had 12,345 students last year. This year, 2,345 students graduated, and 5,678 new students enrolled. How many students are in the school now?
119.	An airplane flew 28,765 kilometers on Monday and 31,567 kilometers on Tuesday. How many kilometers did it fly over both days?
120.	A store had ₹52,345 in sales in one week. It refunded ₹3,456 to customers and earned ₹12,789 in extra sales. How much money does the store have now?
121.	A farm harvested 43,567 kg of wheat and 29,876 kg of rice. How much grain did the farm harvest in total?
123.	A bank had ₹98,765. After giving out loans of ₹12,345 and receiving deposits of ₹8,789, how much money is in the bank?
124.	A train travelled 67,432 kilometers in April and 59,765 kilometers in May. How many kilometers did it travel in both months?
125.	A company had 123,456 products. It sold 67,890 products and manufactured 34,567

	more. How many products does the company have now?
126.	A city spent ₹35,678 on building roads and ₹23,456 on parks. How much did the city spend in total?
127.	A library bought 18,765 new books but removed 5,432 old ones. How many books does the library have now if it originally had 36,789?
128.	A school had ₹78,456 in its budget. It spent ₹12,345 on sports equipment and ₹23,567 on books. How much is left in the budget?
129.	A ship transported 45,678 tons of cargo in March and 38,765 tons in April. How much cargo did it transport in these two months?
130.	A factory manufactured 92,345 units of products and sold 53,678 units. Then, it produced 12,789 more. How many units are left in the factory?
131.	A hospital had 12,345 patients last year. This year, 8,765 patients were discharged, and 9,876 new patients were admitted. How many patients are there now?
132.	A team of workers built 48,765 kilometers of road. Then they repaired 12,345 kilometers and

	constructed 7,890 more. How many kilometers of road were completed?
133.	A car dealership had 23,456 cars. It sold 8,765 cars and received 4,567 new cars. How many cars are there now?
134.	A company had 87,654 employees. 13,567 employees retired, but 9,876 new employees joined. How many employees does the company have now?
135.	A farm produced 78,345 kg of apples and 45,678 kg of oranges. How much fruit did the farm produce in total?
136.	A store had ₹45,678 in earnings. It spent ₹23,456 on new stock and earned an additional ₹12,345. How much money does the store have now?
137.	A publisher printed 12,345 books. It sold 8,567 books and printed 4,789 more. How many books are left now?
138.	A city's population was 123,456. 45,678 people moved out, and 12,345 new people moved in. What is the population now?
139.	A factory produced 67,890 units of a product and shipped out 34,567 units. Then it

	manufactured 9,876 more. How many units does the factory have now?
140.	A businessman earned ₹56,789 in profits and spent ₹23,456 on new investments. He earned another ₹12,345. How much profit does he have now?
141.	A farmer harvested 34,567 kg of wheat and 23,456 kg of corn. How much grain did the farmer harvest in total?
142.	A car rental company had 78,345 cars. It rented out 45,678 and bought 12,345 more. How many cars are in the company now?
143.	A school had 23,456 books in its library. It received 8,765 more books and lost 1,234 books. How many books are in the library now?
144.	A theatre sold 12,345 tickets in the first month and 9,876 tickets in the second month. How many tickets were sold in both months?
145.	A company's revenue was ₹89,765. It spent ₹45,678 on salaries and earned an extra ₹15,678. How much revenue does the company have now?

146.	A zoo had 5,678 animals. It received 1,234 more animals and sent away 876. How many animals are in the zoo now?
147.	A restaurant served 34,567 meals in the first quarter of the year and 29,876 meals in the second quarter. How many meals were served in total?
148.	A bookstore sold 23,456 books in January, then sold 18,765 more in February. How many books did it sell in these two months?
149.	A city park had 45,678 visitors last year. This year, 12,345 more visitors came, but 8,765 fewer attended the events. How many visitors are there this year?
150.	A stadium had 56,789 seats. After renovations, it lost 3,456 seats but added 1,234 new ones. How many seats are there now?
151.	A movie earned ₹45,678 in its first week and ₹34,567 in the second week. What was the total earning?
152.	A train company carried 76,543 passengers last year and 45,678 passengers this year. How many passengers were carried in both years?

153.	A car factory made 123,456 cars, sold 45,678 cars, and produced 9,876 more. How many cars are there now?
154.	A mall had 67,890 visitors last month. This month, it had 45,678 visitors. How many visitors did the mall have in total?
155.	A store earned ₹23,456 on Monday and ₹18,765 on Tuesday. How much money did it earn in both days combined?
156.	A company sold 12,345 laptops in January and 8,765 in February. How many laptops were sold in total?
157.	A farmer grew 23,456 kg of rice and 12,345 kg of wheat. How much grain did the farmer produce altogether?
158.	A school had 5,678 students last year. This year, it gained 1,234 more students but lost 678 students. How many students are in the school now?
159.	A bookstore had 12,345 novels and 8,765 textbooks. How many books did it have in total?

160.	A train travelled 56,789 km in January and 34,567 km in February. How many kilometers did it travel in both months?
161.	A company had ₹67,890 in revenue. It spent ₹45,678 on salaries and earned ₹12,345 more. What is the total revenue now?
162.	A stadium had 23,456 spectators in one event and 18,765 in another. How many spectators were there in total?
163.	A company made 34,567 products in the first quarter and sold 12,345. Then, it made 9,876 more. How many products are left in the company?
164.	A shop earned ₹234,567 on Monday and ₹123,456 on Tuesday. It spent ₹78,900 on inventory. How much profit does the shop have?
165.	A company earned ₹1,234,789 in sales but lost ₹345,678 in a deal. It then earned ₹567,890 from a new contract. What is its current revenue?
166.	A charity received ₹678,345 in donations and spent ₹345,678 on relief work. It received another ₹123,456. How much is left?

167.	A bank had ₹2,345,678 in deposits. After giving out loans of ₹678,456 and receiving deposits of ₹456,789, how much does the bank have now?
168.	A shopkeeper bought products worth ₹567,890. He sold them for ₹789,456 and later spent ₹123,456 on new stock. How much profit did he make?
169.	A company made ₹4,567,890 in profits and invested ₹2,345,678 in a new project. It later earned another ₹1,234,567. What is its final profit?
170.	A person saved ₹567,890. They spent ₹345,678 on a new car and later earned ₹123,456 in interest. How much do they have left?
171.	A hotel earned ₹1,234,567 from bookings but spent ₹678,456 on renovations. It later earned ₹345,678 from additional bookings. How much did it profit?
172.	A bank account had ₹789,456. The owner withdrew ₹234,567 and later deposited ₹123,456. How much is in the account now?

173.	A factory made a profit of ₹3,456,789 but spent ₹1,234,567 on equipment. It earned ₹678,456 more from exports. What is its current profit?
174.	A business had ₹567,890 in its account. It spent ₹345,678 on supplies and then received ₹123,456 in sales. How much is in the account now?
175.	A company made ₹2,345,678 from sales and then spent ₹1,234,567 on expenses. It earned ₹678,901 from another project. What is its total profit now?
176.	A person had ₹987,654 in savings. They spent ₹123,456 on a vacation and later saved ₹234,567. How much money is left?
177.	A charity raised ₹789,456. It spent ₹345,678 on aid programs and received another ₹234,567. How much money does the charity have now?
178.	A store earned ₹456,789 in one week. It spent ₹123,456 on supplies and earned ₹234,567 in extra sales. How much profit is left?
179.	A businessman earned ₹1,234,567 in profit, but lost ₹345,678 in a failed deal. Later, he earned ₹456,789 from another deal. What is his current profit?

180.	A company made ₹2,345,678 in sales and spent ₹1,234,567 on expenses. Then, it earned ₹567,890 more. What is its current profit?
181.	A person saved ₹789,456. They withdrew ₹123,456 for expenses and later saved another ₹234,567. How much money is left in the account?
182.	A bank had ₹3,456,789 in deposits. It gave out loans of ₹1,234,567 and later received ₹567,890 in new deposits. How much money does the bank have now?
183.	A shop earned ₹567,890 from sales. It spent ₹234,567 on new products and earned another ₹123,456 in sales. What is the final profit?
184.	A company had ₹2,345,678 in its account. It spent ₹1,234,567 on a project and earned ₹789,456 from another contract. How much is left in the account?
185.	A business earned ₹1,234,567 in sales but spent ₹678,456 on expenses. Later, it earned ₹345,678 more. What is the total profit now?
186.	A person saved ₹4,567,890. They spent ₹1,234,567 on a house and later saved ₹567,890 more. How much do they have now?

187.	A charity raised ₹567,890. It spent ₹234,567 on a project and later raised another ₹123,456. How much money does it have now?
188.	A store earned ₹3,456,789 in sales. It spent ₹1,234,567 on inventory and later earned ₹567,890 more. How much is the total profit?
189.	A shop earned ₹234,567 on Monday and ₹123,456 on Tuesday. It spent ₹78,900 on inventory. How much profit does the shop have?
190.	A car travelled 34,567 km on Monday and 23,456 km on Tuesday. It then travelled 12,345 km on Wednesday. How far did it travel in total?
191.	A train travelled 78,901 km in January and 56,789 km in February. How far did it travel in both months?
192.	An airplane flew 123,456 km on its first trip and 98,765 km on its second trip. How far did it fly in total?
193.	A truck covered 67,890 km in one month. It travelled another 34,567 km the next month. How far did the truck travel in these two months?

194.	A cyclist rode 12,345 km in the first week, 15,678 km in the second week, and 18,901 km in the third week. What is the total distance travelled?
195.	A ship travelled 45,678 km in April and 34,567 km in May. It then travelled 12,345 km in June. How far did it travel in total?
196.	A bus travelled 23,456 km in January and 19,876 km in February. It then travelled 12,345 km in March. How far did it travel in total?
197.	A marathon runner ran 78,901 km in one month and 56,789 km the next month. How far did the runner travel in total?
198.	A taxi travelled 67,890 km in a year. It travelled 45,678 km the next year. How far did the taxi travel over these two years?
199.	A cyclist rode 23,456 km in the first week, 12,345 km in the second week, and 15,678 km in the third week. How far did the cyclist ride in total?
200.	A plane flew 45,678 km on its first trip, 34,567 km on its second trip, and 12,345 km on its third trip. How far did the plane travel in total?

201.	A truck travelled 123,456 km in one year and 98,765 km the next year. How far did the truck travel over two years?
202.	A ship sailed 78,901 km in one voyage and 56,789 km in another. How far did the ship sail in total?
203.	A train travelled 34,567 km in March, 23,456 km in April, and 12,345 km in May. How far did the train travel in these three months?
204.	A car travelled 45,678 km in one year and 34,567 km the next year. It travelled another 12,345 km in the third year. How far did it travel in total?
205.	A bus travelled 67,890 km in the first six months and 45,678 km in the next six months. How far did it travel in the whole year?
206.	A cyclist rode 23,456 km in January, 34,567 km in February, and 12,345 km in March. How far did the cyclist ride in total?
207.	A plane flew 123,456 km in the first half of the year and 98,765 km in the second half. How far did the plane fly in total?

208.	A train travelled 78,901 km in the first quarter and 56,789 km in the second quarter. How far did it travel in total?
209.	A car travelled 23,456 km in January, 12,345 km in February, and 15,678 km in March. How far did it travel in total?
210.	A ship travelled 45,678 km in one voyage and 34,567 km in another. It then sailed 12,345 km in a third voyage. How far did the ship travel in total?
211.	A bus travelled 123,456 km in one year and 98,765 km the next year. How far did the bus travel in two years?
212.	A cyclist rode 67,890 km in one year and 45,678 km the next year. How far did the cyclist ride over two years?
213.	A train travelled 34,567 km in March, 23,456 km in April, and 12,345 km in May. How far did the train travel over these three months?
214.	A car travelled 45,678 km in one year and 34,567 km the next year. How far did it travel in both years combined?
215.	A car travelled 34,567 km on Monday and 23,456 km on Tuesday. It then travelled 12,345

	km on Wednesday. How far did it travel in total?
216.	A builder constructed 4,567 meters of road in the first phase, 3,456 meters in the second phase, and 2,123 meters in the third phase. What is the total length of the road?
217.	A farm had 12,345 kilograms of wheat. After selling 8,567 kilograms, the farm harvested 5,789 more kilograms. How much wheat does the farm have now?
218.	A factory produced 67,890 liters of paint. After shipping 23,456 liters, it produced another 12,345 liters. How much paint does the factory have now?
219.	A truck transported 56,789 kilograms of goods. After unloading 34,567 kilograms, it picked up 12,345 more kilograms. How much is left on the truck?
220.	A warehouse stored 78,901 kilograms of rice. After selling 45,678 kilograms, it received 23,456 more kilograms. How much rice is in the warehouse now?
221.	A company produced 89,765 meters of fabric. It sold 34,567 meters and manufactured

	another 12,345 meters. How much fabric is left?
222.	Isha bought a candle 10 centimeter and 3 millimetre long. After using it for few days, the length of the candle became 6 millimetres. Find the length of the candle burned out.
223.	A water tank holds 45,678 liters. After using 23,456 liters, it was refilled with 12,345 liters. How much water is in the tank now?
224.	A farmer harvested 56,789 kilograms of corn. After selling 34,567 kilograms, the farmer harvested another 12,345 kilograms. How much corn does the farmer have now?
225.	A pipeline was extended by 12,345 meters in the first phase and 23,456 meters in the second phase. Then, 5,678 meters were added. How long is the pipeline now?
226.	A warehouse received 78,901 kilograms of sugar. After distributing 45,678 kilograms, it received another 12,345 kilograms. How much sugar is in the warehouse now?
227.	A marathon lasted 7 hours 35 minutes. The first runner finished in 2 hours 45 minutes, and

	the second in 3 hours 50 minutes. How much time passed between their finishes?
228.	A train journey takes 15 hours 20 minutes. After 8 hours 45 minutes, it stopped for 2 hours. How long is the remaining journey?
229.	A worker starts at 9:15 AM and works until 4:45 PM, taking a 45-minute break. How many hours does the worker work?
230.	A film lasts 2 hours 45 minutes. After watching for 1 hour 15 minutes, you take a 30-minute break. How much time is left to watch?
231.	A flight took 12 hours 40 minutes. The plane refuelled for 1 hour 20 minutes after flying 7 hours. How long is the remaining flight?
232.	A teacher teaches for 6 hours a day. If she takes breaks totalling 1 hour 15 minutes, how much time does she spend teaching in 5 days?
233.	A bus leaves at 10:30 AM and arrives at 7:15 PM. After driving for 4 hours, the bus stops for 1 hour 30 minutes. How long is the remaining journey?
234.	A worker started at 8:15 AM and finished at 5:30 PM, with 1 hour 10 minutes for lunch. How many hours did the worker work?

235.	A train journey took 9 hours 45 minutes. After 6 hours 20 minutes, the train stopped for 1 hour. How long was the journey after the stop?
236.	A movie lasts 3 hours 25 minutes. After watching for 1 hour 45 minutes, you pause for 20 minutes. How much of the movie is left to watch?
237.	A worker started his shift at 7:30 AM and worked until 5:00 PM, with a 50-minute lunch break. How many hours did he work in total?
238.	A road trip took 10 hours 50 minutes. After driving for 6 hours 20 minutes, the driver stopped for 1 hour 40 minutes. How much time is left to drive?
239.	A concert lasted 4 hours 15 minutes. After 2 hours 30 minutes, there was a 30-minute break. How much time was left after the break?
240.	A movie marathon lasted 9 hours 45 minutes. After 5 hours, there was a 1 hour 15-minute break. How long is the remaining time for the marathon?
241.	A train journey was scheduled for 14 hours 30 minutes. After traveling for 8 hours 20 minutes, it stopped for 1 hour 50 minutes. How long is the rest of the journey?

242.	A plane was in the air for 16 hours 20 minutes. After 10 hours, it stopped to refuel for 1 hour. How long did the rest of the flight take?
243.	A concert started at 5:30 PM and ended at 10:45 PM, with a 25-minute intermission. How long did the concert last?
244.	A worker starts at 6:45 AM and finishes at 3:30 PM, with a 1 hour 15-minute lunch break. How many hours did the worker work?
245.	A sports match lasted 3 hours 40 minutes. After 2 hours 15 minutes, there was a 20-minute break. How much time was left to play?
246.	A train travelled for 13 hours 55 minutes. After 9 hours 30 minutes, the train stopped for 1 hour 25 minutes. How long was the journey after the stop?
247.	A work shift lasts 8 hours 30 minutes. After working for 5 hours 10 minutes, there was a 40-minute break. How much work time was left?
248.	A ship sailed for 18 hours 50 minutes. After 12 hours, it stopped for 1 hour 30 minutes. How long was the remaining journey?
249.	A driver covered a distance of 500 km in 9 hours 45 minutes. After driving for 6 hours, he

	took a 1 hour 15 minutes break. How much time was left for driving?
250.	A conference lasted 6 hours 15 minutes. After 4 hours 30 minutes, there was a 40-minute break. How much time was left after the break?
251.	A person worked for 12 hours 10 minutes, taking two breaks of 30 minutes each. How many hours did the person work without breaks?
252.	A movie lasted 2 hours 50 minutes. After watching for 1 hour 30 minutes, there was a 15-minute break. How much of the movie is left to watch?
253.	A worker starts at 9:10 AM and finishes at 6:30 PM, taking a 1 hour 10 minutes lunch break. How many hours did the worker work?
254.	A concert lasted 5 hours 25 minutes. After 3 hours 10 minutes, there was a 45-minute intermission. How much time was left for the concert after the intermission?
255.	A flight took 14 hours 20 minutes. After flying for 9 hours 15 minutes, the plane refuelled for 1 hour 40 minutes. How long was the remaining flight?

256.	A road trip took 13 hours 45 minutes. After driving for 8 hours, the driver stopped for 2 hours. How much time was left to drive?
257.	A student studies for 7 hours 50 minutes a day. After studying for 4 hours 15 minutes, they took a 30-minute break. How much study time is left?
258.	A flight took 18 hours 30 minutes. After flying for 11 hours 20 minutes, there was a 1 hour 45 minutes refuel stop. How long did the remaining flight take?
259.	A bus journey lasted 9 hours 10 minutes. After traveling for 5 hours 30 minutes, the bus stopped for 40 minutes. How long is the rest of the journey?
260.	A teacher works 7 hours 40 minutes a day. After working for 5 hours, there is a 1 hour 10 minutes meeting. How many hours are left to work after the meeting?
261.	A shift lasts 12 hours 50 minutes. After working for 7 hours 30 minutes, there was a 1 hour 20 minutes break. How much time is left in the shift?

262.	A worker starts at 8:15 AM and finishes at 5:45 PM, with 1 hour lunch break. How many hours did the worker work?
263.	A ship sailed for 16 hours 30 minutes. After sailing for 10 hours, it stopped for 1 hour 50 minutes. How long was the remaining journey?
264.	A sports event lasted 4 hours 55 minutes. After 3 hours 10 minutes, there was a 30-minute break. How much time was left to play after the break?
265.	A worker's shift lasted 9 hours 45 minutes. After working for 6 hours 20 minutes, the worker took an hour break. How much time was left in the shift?
266.	A marathon lasted 6 hours 50 minutes. After 4 hours 30 minutes, there was a 1 hour 10 minutes break. How long was the rest of the marathon?
267.	A factory produces 1,245 toys every day. How many toys does the factory produce in 32 days?
268.	A farmer harvested 2,345 apples from each of his 15 trees. How many apples did he harvest in total?

269.	A school has 1,280 students, and each student is given 5 books. How many books are needed in total?
270.	A delivery truck carries 3,456 boxes of goods per trip. How many boxes are carried after 14 trips?
271.	A printing press prints 1,950 books per day. How many books does it print in 25 days?
272.	A theatre has 2,345 seats, and each seat ticket costs ₹150. How much money will the theatre make if all seats are sold?
273.	A farmer plants 2,240 seeds in each field, and he has 12 fields. How many seeds does the farmer plant in total?
274.	A company sells 1,670 computers, and each computer costs ₹45,000. How much money does the company earn from selling all the computers?
275.	A library has 4,500 bookshelves, and each shelf holds 234 books. How many books are in the library?
276.	A factory produces 1,480 cars each month. How many cars does it produce in 18 months?

277.	A warehouse stores 3,560 units of goods, and each unit weighs 15 kg. What is the total weight of all the goods in the warehouse?
278.	A bakery makes 2,145 cakes every week. How many cakes will the bakery make in 20 weeks?
279.	A farm has 1,850 cows, and each cow produces 12 liters of milk daily. How much milk is produced by all the cows in 30 days?
280.	A truck can carry 1,440 boxes of goods. How many boxes will 25 trucks carry in total?
281.	A stadium has 3,600 seats, and each seat is sold for ₹350. How much money will be made if all seats are sold?
282.	A machine packs 1,680 packets of biscuits every hour. How many packets will the machine pack in 24 hours?
283.	A city has 2,530 streetlights, and each streetlight costs ₹4,000. How much will it cost to replace all the streetlights?
284.	A shop sells 2,145 t-shirts in a month, and each t-shirt costs ₹650. How much does the shop make from selling all the t-shirts?

285.	A farmer grows 1,200 oranges in each orchard, and he has 16 orchards. How many oranges does the farmer grow in total?
286.	A car travels 345 kilometers each day. How many kilometers does it travel in 65 days?
287.	A truck travels 450 kilometers per day. How far will the truck travel in 75 days?
288.	A train covers 678 kilometers per trip. If it makes 20 trips in a month, how many kilometers will it travel in 12 months?
289.	A delivery van travels 89 kilometers on each trip. If it makes 6 trips a day, how far will it travel in 30 days?
290.	A cyclist covers 42 kilometers in one day. How many kilometers will the cyclist cover in 365 days?
291.	A company manufactures 12,456 items daily. Each item costs ₹45. How much does the company earn in 15 days?
292.	A shopkeeper bought a bundle of registers containing one dozen registers for ₹ 699. How much did he pay for one such register?

293.	A shop sells 567 toys each for ₹120. If the shop sells the same number of toys for 30 days, how much money does it make?
294.	A factory produces 24,500 gadgets each month. Each gadget is sold for ₹90. How much does the factory make in 12 months?
295.	A businessman invests ₹65,432 in 8 projects. Each project generates 5 times the amount invested. How much money does he get in total from all projects?
296.	A supermarket sells 1,234 units of a product every day. If each unit costs ₹150, how much does the supermarket earn in 45 days?
297.	A company sells 78,900 mobile phones, each costing ₹12,000. What is the total amount the company earns from selling all phones?
298.	A store earns ₹1,250 daily by selling 250 items. How much does the store earn in a week if each item sells for ₹50?
299.	A bakery sells 425 cakes each day. If each cake is sold for ₹200, how much money does the bakery make in 25 days?

300.	A business sells 5,600 products, each priced at ₹750. How much does it make from the sale of all products?
301.	A car travels 156 kilometers per trip. If the car makes 5 trips in a day, how far will it travel in 45 days?
302.	A bus travels 320 kilometers per day. How many kilometers will it travel in 100 days?
303.	A plane covers 12,000 kilometers on each flight. How many kilometers will it cover in 150 flights?
304.	A train travels 780 kilometers per day. How many kilometers will it travel in 60 days?
305.	A truck travels 980 kilometers daily. How many kilometers will it travel in 90 days?
306.	A bookstore sells 789 books daily. Each book costs ₹350. How much does the store earn in 60 days?
307.	A factory produces 1,500 gadgets each day. Each gadget is sold for ₹110. How much will the factory make in 40 days?
308.	A company makes 23,500 products, each of which sells for ₹300. How much money does the company make from the products?

309.	A worker earns ₹650 per hour and works for 7 hours a day. How much does the worker earn in 30 days?
310.	A farmer sells 8,500 kilograms of wheat at ₹45 per kilogram. How much does the farmer make from the sale of all the wheat?
311.	A manufacturer produces 10,400 widgets daily, each priced at ₹85. How much will the company earn in a year (365 days)?
312.	A shop sells 1,236 boxes of chocolates at ₹210 per box. What is the total revenue from selling all the chocolates?
313.	A delivery company charges ₹750 per delivery. If the company makes 245 deliveries in a month, how much money does it earn in 3 months?
314.	A business sells 15,678 laptops, each priced at ₹55,000. What is the total revenue from selling all laptops?
315.	A factory produces 13,500 toys each week. Each toy sells for ₹75. How much money will the factory make in 8 weeks?

316.	A factory operates for 1,250 hours each month. How many hours does it operate in 18 months?
317.	A train travels 1,980 kilometers every day. How far does it travel in 45 days?
318.	A machine runs for 2,600 hours per year. How many hours will it run in 12 years?
319.	A worker works for 1,560 hours each year. How many hours will the worker work in 25 years?
320.	A bus travels 2,150 kilometers per day. How far will it travel in 90 days?
321.	A marathon runner trains for 1,200 hours each year. How many hours will the runner train in 8 years?
322.	Dino's mother left for Delhi on June 2 and returned on August 10 of the same year. How many days did she stay in Delhi if the 2nd June and 1oth of August are not included?
323.	A ship sails 3,500 kilometers every week. How far will it sail in 3 months?
324.	A factory produces goods for 2,400 hours every year. How many hours will it produce goods in 15 years?

325.	A delivery truck drives 1,950 kilometers each day. How far will the truck travel in 60 days?
326.	A plane flies 3,200 kilometers per hour. How far will it fly in 18 hours?
327.	A worker works 2,080 hours every year. How many hours will the worker work in 6 years?
328.	A car travels 2,150 kilometers per week. How far will it travel in 52 weeks?
329.	A machine operates for 1,680 hours per year. How many hours will it operate in 10 years?
330.	A cyclist rides 1,900 kilometers in a month. How far will the cyclist ride in 4years?
331.	A factory operates for 1,540 hours every year. How many hours will it operate in 20 years?
332.	A train travels 2,150 kilometers per day. How many kilometers will it cover in 18 days?
333.	A plane covers 3,400 kilometers per hour. How many kilometers will it fly in 9 hours?
334.	A factory runs 1,200 hours per year. How many hours will it run in 7 years?
335.	A delivery truck travels 1,860 kilometers every day. How many kilometers will it cover in 14 days?

336.	A machine operates 1,750 hours per year. How many hours will it operate in 12 years?
337.	A cyclist rides 1,345 kilometers in a week. How many kilometers will the cyclist ride in 8 weeks?
338.	A car travels 2,000 kilometers per trip. How many kilometers will it travel in 10 trips?
339.	A bus travels 1,780 kilometers every day. How many kilometers will it travel in 20 days?
340.	A boat travels 1,850 kilometers per week. How many kilometers will it travel in 1 year?
341.	A grocery store receives 50 boxes of apples. Each box contains 12 apples. They sell 150 apples and then restock with 5 more boxes of apples. How many apples are in the store now?
342.	Sam's bakery makes 30 cakes each day. After 3 days, they sell 65 cakes and receive an order for 24 more. How many cakes are left after these transactions?
343.	A school has 450 students. Each class has 25 students. After some students graduate, 4 new classes of 30 students each are added. How many students are there now?

344.	A farmer plants 80 rows of corn. Each row contains 50 corn plants. 20 rows are destroyed by pests, but he plants 10 more rows of 60 plants each. How many corn plants are there now?
345.	A construction company has 15 workers. Each worker can build 3 houses in a month. After 2 months, 5 workers leave, but the company hires 8 more. How many houses can the company build in the next month?
346.	A zoo has 8 enclosures with 12 animals each. They move 3 animals from each enclosure to a different zoo, then receive 4 more enclosures with 10 animals each. How many animals are in the zoo now?
347.	John has $500. He buys 3 video games costing $40 each, sells 2 old games for $25 each, and then buys 4 books costing $15 each. How much money does he have left?
348.	A factory produces 600 toys. They sell 120 toys, then produce 80 more each day for 5 days. How many toys does the factory have after 5 days?
349.	A furniture store has 300 chairs. They sell 60 chairs, then make 15 more chairs each day for

	6 days. After that, they sell 80 more chairs. How many chairs remain?
350.	A company hires 12 employees. Each employee earns \$2,000 per month. After 3 months, 3 employees leave, but the company hires 5 new employees who earn \$1,800 each. How much does the company pay its employees in the 4th month?
351.	A farmer has 300 cows. Each cow produces 10 liters of milk daily. After 4 days, 20 cows are sold, and the remaining cows produce milk for 3 more days. How many liters of milk have been produced in total?
352.	A construction crew builds 5 houses in 2 months, using 1,000 bricks per house. They receive an order for 3 more houses, each requiring 1,200 bricks. If they have 15,000 bricks, how many bricks will they need to purchase?
353.	A gardener has 150 plants. Each plant produces 5 flowers daily. After 6 days, 30 plants are removed, and the remaining plants continue to produce flowers for 4 more days. How many flowers have been produced in total?

354.	A factory has 50 machines. Each machine makes 200 products daily. After 3 days, 5 machines break down, and the remaining machines work for 2 more days. How many products have been made in total?
355.	A farmer owns 120 hens. Each hen lays 3 eggs per day. After 5 days, 20 hens are sold, and the remaining hens continue to lay eggs for 6 more days. How many eggs were laid in total?
356.	A rancher has 250 sheep. Each sheep produces 4 kilograms of wool every week. After 2 weeks, 40 sheep are sold, and the remaining sheep produce wool for 3 more weeks. How many kilograms of wool have been produced?
357.	A factory has 20 workers. Each worker assembles 30 gadgets per day. After 7 days, 4 workers leave, and the remaining workers continue assembling gadgets for 5 more days. How many gadgets have been assembled in total?
358.	A school cafeteria serves 150 students daily. Each student receives 2 meals per day. After 4 days, 50 students leave for a trip, and the remaining students continue receiving meals

	for 3 more days. How many meals were served in total?
359.	A publishing house has 40 writers. Each writer produces 5 pages per day. After 6 days, 10 writers take a leave, and the remaining writers continue working for 4 more days. How many pages have been produced in total?
360.	A baker has 60 ovens. Each oven bakes 15 loaves of bread daily. After 5 days, 10 ovens break down, and the remaining ovens continue to bake for 3 more days. How many loaves of bread were baked in total?
361.	A factory has 100 workers. Each worker makes 8 products daily. After 5 days, 20 workers are transferred to another department, and the remaining workers continue for 6 more days. How many products have been made?
362.	A dairy farm has 80 cows. Each cow produces 12 liters of milk per day. After 3 days, 10 cows are sold, and the remaining cows produce milk for 5 more days. How many liters of milk have been produced in total?
363.	A gardener has 150 plants. Each plant produces 5 flowers daily. After 6 days, 30 plants are removed, and the remaining plants continue to produce flowers for 4 more days.

	How many flowers have been produced in total?
364.	John has 100,000 marbles. He wants to share them equally with 5 friends. How many marbles will each friend get?
365.	A company printed 500,000 flyers. They want to distribute them equally to 10 stores. How many flyers will each store get?
366.	There are 600,000 apples packed in 15 large boxes. How many apples are in each box?
367.	A library has 800,000 books and wants to place them evenly across 20 shelves. How many books will go on each shelf?
368.	A baker baked 1,000 cookies and wants to pack them into boxes, with each box containing 50 cookies. How many boxes are needed?
369.	A city built 1,200 houses. They plan to divide them equally into 30 neighbourhoods. How many houses will each neighbourhood have?
370.	A company manufactured 2,000 bicycles. They want to ship them to 4 different countries. How many bicycles will each country receive?

371.	A school has 3,000,000 pencils. They are distributing them equally to 60 classes. How many pencils will each class get?
372.	A farmer harvested 4,500 strawberries. He packed them into boxes, with each box holding 50 strawberries. How many boxes did he pack?
373.	There are 5,000,000 candies in a factory, and they need to be equally divided among 100 stores. How many candies will each store receive?
374.	A zoo has 10,000,000 visitors every year, and they want to equally distribute the visitors over 365 days. How many visitors does the zoo get per day?
375.	A stadium can hold 15,000,000 spectators in a year. If the stadium hosts 30 games, how many people attend each game on average?
376.	A scientist collected 1,500,000 insects and divided them into 15 groups for research. How many insects are in each group?
377.	Find the number of years in 3192 months and the number of weeks in 3192 days.
378.	A train can carry 8,000,000 kilograms of goods. If each trip carries 40 kilograms, how many trips are needed to carry all the goods?

379.	A city produced 20,000,000 liters of water in a month. They distributed it equally to 20 buildings. How much water did each building get?
380.	A company sold 12,000,000 toys over 60 days. How many toys did they sell each day?
381.	A farmer harvested 25,000 grains of wheat. He packed them into 50 bags. How many grains are in each bag?
382.	An airline has 9,000 passengers each year. If there are 30 days of flights, how many passengers fly per day?
383.	A factory made 30,000 chocolate bars. They want to pack them equally into 60 boxes. How many chocolate bars will go into each box?
384.	A school cafeteria serves 7,500 meals in a year. If they serve meals on 15 school days, how many meals are served each day?
385.	Anya has ₹3.50. She finds another ₹2.25 in her bag. How many paise does she have in total?
386.	Rohan saved ₹8 and his friend gave him another ₹3.75. How much does Rohan have in paise?

387.	Meera bought candies for ₹6.25. How much did she spend in paise?
388.	A chocolate costs ₹4.75, and Sam bought two of them. How much did he spend in paise?
389.	If a pencil costs ₹1.15, how many paise would 5 pencils cost?
390.	A book costs ₹120.50, and a notebook costs ₹35.25. How much will both items cost together?
391.	Neha bought a pen for ₹15.75 and an eraser for ₹5.50. If she paid ₹50, how much change did she get back?
392.	Rina spent ₹45 on a doll and ₹39.50 on a ball. How much did she spend in total?
393.	Suresh has ₹100, and he spent ₹75.25 on a toy. How much money does he have left?
394.	A shirt costs ₹250.75, and a trouser costs ₹199.90. How much do they cost together?
395.	Riya buys 3 toys, each costing ₹17.50. How much does she spend in total?
396.	A bottle of juice costs ₹22.50. How much will 4 bottles cost?

397.	If one chocolate costs ₹12.75, how much will 6 chocolates cost?
398.	A pencil costs ₹5.25. How much would 10 pencils cost?
399.	Raj buys 8 notebooks at ₹9.75 each. What is his total cost?
400.	Sahil has ₹60, and he wants to divide it equally among 5 friends. How much will each friend get?
401.	A box of cookies costs ₹100, and it has 10 cookies. What is the cost of each cookie?
402.	A fruit seller made ₹150 by selling 6 boxes of fruits. How much did he earn from each box?
403.	A water bottle costs ₹45 for a pack of 3. What is the price of one water bottle?
404.	Aarav has ₹120, and he needs to buy pencils that cost ₹5 each. How many pencils can he buy?
405.	Naina has ₹200. She buys a pen for ₹25.75, a notebook for ₹55.50, and a sharpener for ₹10. How much money does she have left?

406.	Arjun sold 10 bottles of lemonade for ₹15 each. He spent ₹30 on lemons. What was his profit?
407.	Tina has ₹150. She buys chocolates at ₹12 each. How many chocolates can she buy, and how much money will she have left?
408.	A sandwich costs ₹25, and a juice costs ₹15. A group of 5 friends each buy one sandwich and one juice. What is the total cost for the group?
409.	Rishi bought 3 shirts at ₹120 each and 2 pairs of shoes at ₹250 each. How much did he spend in total?
410.	Priya bought a gift for ₹50.75, a card for ₹15.50, and wrapping paper for ₹10. She paid with a ₹100 note. How much change did she get?
411.	Four friends contributed equally to buy a gift worth ₹160. How much did each friend contribute?
412.	A shopkeeper has ₹500. He needs to give 5 customers an equal amount of ₹50 each. How much money will he have left after giving to all the customers?

413.	Alia bought a bracelet for ₹75. If she saves ₹15 per day, how many days will it take her to save enough to buy two more bracelets?
414.	Ramesh spent ₹230 on groceries and ₹175 on clothes. If he had ₹500 at the start, how much money does he have now?
415.	Amit found ₹7.85 in his pocket and later borrowed ₹4.15 from his friend. How much money does Amit have in paise?
416.	A notebook costs ₹12.60, and its cover costs ₹3.40. How many paise would it cost to buy both the notebook and its cover?
417.	Kavya has ₹15.50 in her piggy bank, and her mom gives her an additional ₹5.25. How many paise does she have now?
418.	Maya bought a packet of chips for ₹9.75 and a juice box for ₹6.50. How much did she spend in total in paise?
419.	If one cupcake costs ₹3.20, how many paise would 7 cupcakes cost?
420.	How many 25-paise coins make up ₹5?
421.	If you have ten 50-paise coins, how many rupees do you have?

422.	How many 10-paise coins are needed to make ₹2.50?
423.	Rohan has three 1-rupee coins and two 50-paise coins. How much money does he have in total?
424.	How many 20-paise coins would you need to equal ₹4?
425.	Priya has four 25-paise coins and five 50-paise coins. How much does she have altogether in rupees?
426.	If each chocolate costs ₹1.50, how many 50-paise coins does Rina need to buy two chocolates?
427.	How many 1-rupee coins and 50-paise coins together make ₹6 if the number of 1-rupee coins is three times the number of 50-paise coins?
428.	Aarav has ₹10 in 2-rupee coins and 50-paise coins. If he has twice as many 2-rupee coins as 50-paise coins, how many coins of each type does he have?
429.	How many 5-paise coins would you need to collect ₹1.25?

430.	Priya has three times as many 25-paise coins as 50-paise coins. The total value of her coins is ₹10. How many coins of each type does she have?
431.	Rohan has some ₹5 notes and ₹10 notes. If he has 12 notes in total with a combined value of ₹85, how many notes of each denomination does he have?
432.	Meera's coin collection includes only 1-rupee, 50-paise, and 25-paise coins. She has a total of 30 coins, and their combined value is ₹18. If she has twice as many 1-rupee coins as 50-paise coins, how many of each type does she have?
433.	In a piggy bank, there are only 10-paise and 25-paise coins. The number of 25-paise coins is 10 more than twice the number of 10-paise coins. If the total value of the coins is ₹10, how many coins of each type are there?
434.	A shopkeeper has 3 times as many 2-rupee coins as 1-rupee coins and twice as many 50-paise coins as 1-rupee coins. If the total value of all coins is ₹20, how many of each type of coin does he have?

435.	Anya buys 5 pens and 3 notebooks. The total cost is ₹150. If each notebook costs ₹20 more than each pen, what is the price of one pen?
436.	Kabir has ₹500, and he wants to buy pens that cost ₹12 each and erasers that cost ₹5 each. If he buys twice as many pens as erasers, how many of each can he buy while spending exactly ₹500?
437.	A bag of apples costs ₹120, and a bag of oranges costs ₹90. If Arjun buys twice as many bags of oranges as apples and spends a total of ₹1,020, how many bags of each did he buy?
438.	Seema and her friends pooled their money to buy a gift for ₹240. If each friend contributed ₹10 more than the friend before, and Seema contributed the least at ₹20, how many friends contributed to the gift?
439.	A store sells notebooks at ₹15 each and pencils at ₹8 each. John spent ₹120 in total, buying twice as many pencils as notebooks. How many notebooks and pencils did he buy?
440.	A cashier has a drawer containing 100 coins in 1-rupee, 2-rupee, and 5-rupee denominations. The total value of the coins is ₹200, and there are twice as many 1-rupee coins as 5-rupee

	coins. How many coins of each denomination are there?
441.	Alisha has only ₹10 and ₹20 notes in her purse. If she has 15 notes totalling ₹220, how many notes of each denomination does she have?
442.	A vending machine has 50 coins in 1-rupee, 2-rupee, and 5-rupee denominations, with a combined value of ₹90. If there are twice as many 2-rupee coins as 1-rupee coins, find the number of coins of each type.
443.	In a wallet, there are ₹100 in 10-rupee and 20-rupee notes. If there are 7 notes in total, how many of each type of note are there?
444.	A bag contains only ₹1, ₹2, and ₹5 coins. The total number of coins is 60, and the total value is ₹150. If the number of ₹2 coins is equal to the number of ₹5 coins, how many of each type of coin does the bag contain?
445.	Mira spends ₹500 buying some notebooks and pens. If each notebook costs ₹20 and each pen costs ₹15, and she buys twice as many pens as notebooks, how many of each did she buy?

446.	Rishi has ₹500 in 20-rupee and 50-rupee notes. If he has 15 notes in total and twice as many 20-rupee notes as 50-rupee notes, how many notes of each type does he have?
447.	A school trip costs ₹5,000 in total. If 5 friends contributed equal amounts and the remaining cost was divided equally among 10 other friends, how much did each group of friends contribute?
448.	An ice cream vendor has a collection of coins totalling ₹100. He has an equal number of 50-paise, ₹1, and ₹2 coins. How many coins of each type does he have?
449.	A total of ₹300 is collected from the sale of pencils at ₹2 each and pens at ₹5 each. If 100 items were sold in total, how many pencils and pens were sold?
450.	A shape has 4 sides of equal length and opposite sides are parallel. What shape could this be?
451.	A figure has 5 sides and 5 vertices. What is the name of this shape?
452.	Which of the following shapes has all sides equal and all angles equal: rectangle, square, or triangle?

453.	You have a triangle where two of its sides are equal. What is this type of triangle called?
454.	A shape has 4 right angles and opposite sides that are equal in length. What shape is it?
455.	If you fold a square paper in half, what new shape will you get?
456.	A hexagon has 6 sides. If you remove 2 of its sides, how many sides does it have now?
457.	A rectangle has a length of 8 cm and a width of 4 cm. What shape would you get if you connected the midpoints of each side of the rectangle?
458.	A triangle has angles of 50° and 70°. What is the measure of its third angle?
459.	If two shapes have the same size and same shape, what are they called?
460.	A rectangle has a length of 12 cm and a width of 5 cm. What is its perimeter?
461.	A square has a side length of 6 cm. What is its perimeter?
462.	The perimeter of a triangle is 18 cm, and two of its sides measure 6 cm and 5 cm. How long is the third side?

463.	A garden is in the shape of a rectangle, with a length of 10 m and a width of 7 m. What is the area of the garden?
464.	The side length of a square is doubled. How many times greater is the new perimeter compared to the original?
465.	A triangle has two sides that are both 5 cm, and the third side is 8 cm. What is its perimeter?
466.	A rectangle has a perimeter of 20 cm. If the width is 4 cm, what is its length?
467.	If the side length of a square is 9 cm, what is its area?
468.	A piece of ribbon forms a square with a perimeter of 36 cm. What is the length of each side?
469.	The area of a rectangle is 24 square cm, and its width is 3 cm. What is its length?
470.	How many right angles are there in a square?
471.	A triangle has one right angle and two equal angles. What are the measures of the two equal angles?

472.	If a line is drawn through the middle of a circle, dividing it into two equal halves, what is this line called?
473.	What is the sum of the angles in any triangle?
474.	How many degrees are there in a straight angle?
475.	A rectangle has 4 right angles. If you divide it into two equal triangles, what will be the measure of each angle in these triangles?
476.	How many right angles are there in an octagon?
477.	A circle has a radius of 5 cm. What would be the length of its diameter?
478.	If you have an equilateral triangle, what is the measure of each angle?
479.	In a quadrilateral, two angles are 90° and 120°. If the third angle is 70°, what is the measure of the fourth angle?
480.	A shape has four equal sides but no right angles. What is this shape called?
481.	If you connect any two opposite corners of a rectangle, what shape is formed inside the rectangle?

482.	A circle is divided into 4 equal parts. What is each part called?
483.	How many sides does a decagon have?
484.	Which of the following shapes has no corners: square, circle, or triangle?
485.	If you cut a rectangle along one of its diagonals, how many triangles do you get?
486.	How many lines of symmetry does a square have?
487.	In a regular hexagon, how many equal sides does it have?
488.	If a pentagon has 5 equal sides and 5 equal angles, what is this type of pentagon called?
489.	How many faces does a cube have?
490.	The side length of a square is 4 cm. If you triple the side length, what will be the new perimeter?
491.	A rectangle has a length of 9 cm and a width of 3 cm. If the width is doubled, what will be the new perimeter?
492.	If the side length of a square is 7 cm, what is the perimeter of two such squares placed side by side?

493.	A triangle has side lengths of 4 cm, 6 cm, and 8 cm. If each side is doubled, what is the new perimeter?
494.	A rectangular field has a length of 15 m and a width of 10 m. What is the area of the field?
495.	A classroom wall is shaped like a rectangle with a length of 6 m and a width of 4 m. If you cover the wall with square tiles of side 1 m, how many tiles do you need?
496.	A square has a perimeter of 28 cm. What is the length of each side?
497.	The perimeter of an equilateral triangle is 21 cm. What is the length of each side?
498.	If a garden is in the shape of a rectangle with a perimeter of 60 m and a width of 10 m, what is its length?
499.	Riya recorded the number of cars passing her house in an hour. She made 3 groups of 5 tallies and 2 extra tallies. How many cars passed her house?
500.	In a game, Rohan scored 18 points. He used tally marks to count his points. How many groups of 5 did he make, and how many tallies were left over?

501.	Neha counted the birds she saw in a park. She made 4 groups of 5 tallies and had 1 tally left over. How many birds did she count in total?
502.	A class of students took turns skipping rope. Altogether, they made 2 groups of 5 tallies and 3 extra tallies. How many turns were taken?
503.	Meera recorded the number of buses passing by in a day. She made 5 groups of 5 tallies. How many buses did she count?
504.	Ananya counted the number of apples in two baskets. In the first basket, she made 3 groups of 5 tallies and 2 extra. In the second basket, she made 2 groups of 5 tallies and 4 extra. How many apples were in both baskets together?
505.	Jay used tally marks to count his toy cars. He made 4 groups of 5 tallies and 1 extra tally. He gave away 7 toy cars to his friends. How many toy cars does he have now?
506.	A teacher counted her students using tallies. She recorded 3 groups of 5 tallies. Then, 6 more students joined the class. How many students are there in total?
507.	Sia made 5 groups of 5 tallies while counting her marbles. She then lost 6 marbles. How many marbles does she have left?

508.	A shopkeeper counted 4 groups of 5 tallies for the candies on his shelf. He sold 3 candies. How many are left?
509.	Ananya counted 17 birds and drew tally marks. Jay counted 23 birds and drew tally marks. Who drew more groups of 5, and by how many?
510.	A boy made 3 groups of 5 tallies and 4 extra tallies for his stickers. His friend made 4 groups of 5 tallies and 1 extra tally. Who has more stickers?
511.	One store sold 2 groups of 5 tallies of apples and another store sold 3 groups of 5 tallies of apples. Which store sold more apples, and by how many?
512.	Maya counted 2 groups of 5 tallies and 3 extra tallies for the books she read, while Priya counted 4 groups of 5 tallies. Who read more books?
513.	In a library, there are 6 groups of 5 tallies for mystery books and 8 groups of 5 tallies for adventure books. How many more adventure books are there than mystery books?
514.	A teacher used 3 groups of 5 tallies to count her pencils. If each pencil pack contains twice

	as many pencils as counted, how many pencils are there in total?
515.	Neel counted 2 groups of 5 tallies and 4 extra for his crayons. If he bought twice that amount, how many crayons will he have now?
516.	A student made 4 groups of 5 tallies for the number of papers. If each paper has 3 questions, how many questions are there in total?
517.	A baker counted 3 groups of 5 tallies and 2 extra tallies for cupcakes. If he makes 5 times that amount each week, how many cupcakes does he make in a week?
518.	Riya drew 2 groups of 5 tallies to count the lemons on a tree. If she picks three times that amount, how many lemons will she have?
519.	A class tracked the number of sunny days in a month. They made 6 groups of 5 tallies and 1 extra tally. How many sunny days were there in total?
520.	In a zoo, 3 groups of 5 tallies were made for lions and 4 groups of 5 tallies for tigers. How many big cats are there in total?
521.	A gardener counted 3 groups of 5 tallies and 1 extra tally for flowers in one garden bed and 2

	groups of 5 tallies in another. How many flowers are there altogether?
522.	A farmer recorded the number of eggs his hens laid in one day. He made 7 groups of 5 tallies. If the hens laid 5 more eggs the next day, how many eggs were laid in total?
523.	A store owner counted customers using tallies. She made 6 groups of 5 tallies and 3 extra tallies. How many customers visited her store?
524.	In a survey, 5 groups of 5 tallies were recorded for students who liked chocolate ice cream, and 3 groups of 5 tallies for vanilla ice cream. How many more students preferred chocolate?
525.	A class kept track of books read in a week. They made 4 groups of 5 tallies and 2 extra tallies. How many books were read that week?
526.	A coach tracked the number of times each student completed a lap around the track. If she made 8 groups of 5 tallies, how many laps were run in total?
527.	An artist counted the number of drawings she finished each day. By the end of the month, she had 7 groups of 5 tallies and 3 extra tallies. How many drawings did she complete?

528.	A restaurant tracked the number of sandwiches sold during lunch. They recorded 3 groups of 5 tallies and 2 extra tallies. If the next day they sold twice as many sandwiches, how many sandwiches did they sell on both days?
529.	Sam counted his coins and recorded 2 groups of 5 tallies and 4 extra tallies. If he lost 6 coins, how many tallies would he have left?
530.	A class tracked attendance for a week. They made 4 groups of 5 tallies on Monday and 3 groups of 5 tallies on Tuesday. If 2 more students were present on Wednesday than on Monday, how many tallies would there be on Wednesday?
531.	Jenny used tally marks to record points in a game. She made 5 groups of 5 tallies and 1 extra tally. If she loses 3 points, how many tallies would she have left?
532.	A store recorded toy sales with tally marks. They made 4 groups of 5 tallies on Saturday and 3 groups on Sunday. If they sold twice as many toys on Monday as they did on Sunday, how many toys were sold on Monday?
533.	An animal shelter used tally marks to record the dogs they adopted out. They made 6

	groups of 5 tallies for the first week. If they adopt out 4 more dogs the next week, how many dogs will be adopted out in total?
534.	A school used tally marks to count attendees at a fair. They made 9 groups of 5 tallies. If 7 more people attended after the tally, what is the total attendance?
535.	Lisa recorded her steps using tally marks. She made 4 groups of 5 tallies and 2 extra tallies. If she walks 8 more steps, how many steps would she have recorded?
536.	A book club recorded the number of chapters read by members using tally marks. They made 5 groups of 5 tallies. If the club reads 6 more chapters, how many tally marks would there be in total?
537.	A fruit vendor made tally marks to count the apples sold. He made 3 groups of 5 tallies and 3 extra tallies. If he sells 4 more apples, how many tally marks would he have in total?
538.	A teacher tracked student attendance for 2 days. On Monday, she made 5 groups of 5 tallies, and on Tuesday, she made 6 groups of 5 tallies and 1 extra tally. What is the total attendance for the two days?

539.	Sara started reading at 3:15 PM and read for 45 minutes. What time did she finish reading?
540.	Ravi's train left the station at 10:30 AM and arrived at 1:15 PM. How long was the train journey?
541.	Amy went to play at 2:45 PM and came home at 4:30 PM. How long was she playing outside?
542.	If a movie starts at 6:20 PM and ends at 8:05 PM, how long is the movie?
543.	Maya's favourite show starts at 4:30 PM and lasts 50 minutes. If she starts watching it from the beginning, what time will it end?
544.	A clock shows 2:30 PM. If it takes Ron 1 hour and 20 minutes to complete his homework, what time will it be when he finishes?
545.	Emma's class starts at 9:00 AM and ends at 11:30 AM. How long is her class?
546.	Raj starts studying at 3:15 PM and finishes at 5:00 PM. How much time did he spend studying?
547.	A bus leaves the station at 7:15 AM and arrives at its destination at 9:45 AM. How long is the bus ride?

548.	If a flight departs at 10:20 PM and takes 2 hours and 40 minutes, what time will it land?
549.	How many minutes are there in 4 hours?
550.	Nina read for 3 hours on Saturday. How many minutes did she spend reading?
551.	Jake's workout routine lasts 2 hours and 30 minutes. How many total minutes does he spend working out?
552.	A class lasts for 1 hour and 45 minutes. How many minutes is that in total?
553.	If a workshop takes 5 hours, how many minutes is the workshop?
554.	Aman practices guitar for 6 hours every weekend. How many minutes does he practice each weekend?
555.	A concert is 2 hours and 15 minutes long. How many minutes is this in total?
556.	Tina works 7 hours each day. How many minutes does she work in one day?
557.	A movie is 3 hours and 20 minutes long. Convert this time into minutes.
558.	How many minutes are in 12 hours?

559.	How many seconds are there in 8 minutes?
560.	A quick workout lasts for 10 minutes. How many seconds does it last?
561.	A recipe requires you to boil water for 5 minutes. How many seconds should you boil the water?
562.	If a car race lasts 12 minutes, how many seconds long is the race?
563.	Tom has to hold a yoga pose for 6 minutes. How many seconds is this?
564.	A song lasts for 4 minutes and 30 seconds. Convert the 4 minutes into seconds and add it to 30 seconds.
565.	John took a break for 7 minutes and 15 seconds. How many seconds was his break?
566.	Rishi converted the 12-hour clock time of 2:45 p.m. to 24- hour clock time as 13:45. Is he correct? If not then why?
567.	A time trial race takes 15 minutes. How many seconds is this?
568.	An event lasts 2 minutes and 40 seconds. Convert the 2 minutes into seconds and find the total time in seconds.

569.	How many seconds are there in 20 minutes?
570.	If each exercise in a workout routine takes 3 minutes and there are 10 exercises, how long is the entire workout?
571.	A baker bakes 15 cakes, and each cake takes 25 minutes to bake. How many minutes in total does he spend baking?
572.	A child skips rope for 2 minutes each day. If she skips for 30 days, how many minutes did she skip in total?
573.	A teacher spends 4 minutes with each student. If there are 18 students, how many minutes does she spend in total?
574.	Each lesson at a school is 40 minutes long. If there are 6 lessons in a day, how much time do students spend in lessons each day?
575.	A bird sings for 3 minutes every morning. How many minutes does it sing over a week?
576.	If a worker takes 7 minutes to make one toy, how many minutes will he take to make 25 toys?
577.	A train journey takes 3 hours each day. How many hours will the journey take over a 5-day period?

578.	A video game level takes 15 minutes to complete. If you play 8 levels, how long did you play?
579.	A meeting lasts 30 minutes, and there are 5 meetings in a day. How many minutes do the meetings take in total?
580.	If an event takes 120 minutes and there are 6 sections, how long is each section?
581.	A runner completes a race in 150 seconds, running at the same speed. If there are 5 laps, how many seconds does each lap take?
582.	Rina takes 180 minutes to read a book. If she reads the book over 3 days equally, how many minutes does she read per day?
583.	A teacher gives a 240-minute lecture in 4 parts. How long is each part?
584.	A project is planned to take 360 minutes over 6 days. How many minutes should be worked on each day?
585.	A movie marathon lasts 600 minutes and includes 5 movies. If each movie is the same length, how many minutes is each movie?
586.	A concert runs for 180 minutes, split into 3 equal parts. How long is each part?

587.	If a lecture series lasts 480 minutes and there are 8 lectures, how many minutes is each lecture?
588.	An exam is 75 minutes long and has 5 sections. If each section takes the same time, how long is each section?
589.	A team practices for 150 minutes in 3 equal sessions. How many minutes is each session?
590.	A train leaves the station at 6:20 AM and arrives at its destination at 12:50 PM. If it makes three stops of 15 minutes each, how much time does it actually spend travelling?
591.	Liam studied for a total of 5 hours and 20 minutes across four days. If he studied for the same amount of time each day, how many minutes did he study daily?
592.	Two friends, Ayesha and Bella, plan to meet at the park. Ayesha leaves home at 2:15 PM and arrives at the park 40 minutes later. Bella leaves 20 minutes after Ayesha but reaches the park 15 minutes before her. At what time did Bella reach the park?
593.	James started his workout at 7:50 AM and finished at 9:05 AM. Later that day, he went for another workout for half the duration of the

	morning workout. What time did he finish his second workout if he started it at 6:00 PM?
594.	A marathon started at 8:00 AM, and the first runner finished at 9:37 AM. If the second runner took 7 minutes more than the first, at what time did the second runner finish?
595.	Sarah's flight from Mumbai to Delhi took 2 hours and 15 minutes, and her return flight took 20 minutes longer. If her flight to Mumbai left Delhi at 1:30 PM, at what time did it arrive in Mumbai?
596.	A movie starts at 7:25 PM and ends at 10:05 PM, including a 15-minute break in the middle. How long is the movie without the break?
597.	In a chess tournament, each match lasts 1 hour and 15 minutes. If a player participates in 6 matches with a 30-minute break after each match, how much total time does he spend in the tournament?
598.	A clock gains 3 minutes every hour. If it shows the correct time at 7:00 AM, what time will it show 6 hours later?
599.	Tom and Lily are running a race. Tom takes 20 seconds longer than Lily to complete each lap of the track. If Lily runs a lap in 80 seconds and

	they both run 5 laps, how much total time does Tom take to finish all 5 laps?
600.	A movie starts at 3:45 PM and is 2 hours and 35 minutes long. If there are two 10-minute commercials at the beginning and a 15-minute break in the middle, what time does the movie end?
601.	An athlete runs 10 kilometers in 40 minutes. If she keeps the same speed, how many minutes will it take her to run 15 kilometers?
602.	A clock takes 12 seconds to chime 6 times at 6 o'clock. Assuming the time between each chime is the same, how long will it take to chime 12 times at 12 o'clock?
603.	A chef takes 15 minutes to prepare one pizza. If he has 1 hour and 45 minutes available, what is the maximum number of pizzas he can prepare?
604.	A library opens at 9:30 AM and closes at 5:15 PM. During a special event, it stayed open for an additional 2 hours. If each visitor spent an average of 45 minutes in the library, how many visitors could it accommodate in that time?
605.	A bike race takes 3 hours and 40 minutes for the winner to complete. If the second-place

	finisher takes 15% longer, how much time does the second-place finisher take?
606.	During a hiking trip, a group travelled for 2 hours at 3 km/hr, took a 30-minute break, then walked another hour at 4 km/hr. How far did they hike in total?
607.	A car covers a distance of 150 kilometers in 2 hours and 30 minutes. If the car's speed increases by 20 km/hr, how long will it take to cover the same distance?
608.	Emma has 6 hours to complete a 1200-piece puzzle. If she finishes 450 pieces in the first 2 hours, what is her average time per piece for the remaining pieces to complete the puzzle on time?
609.	A clock shows the time as 11:30 AM. If it runs 1 minute slower every 10 minutes, what time will it actually be when the clock shows 12:30 PM?
610.	Jake's birthday is on June 15. If today is May 20, how many days are left until his birthday?
611.	If today is March 5 and Sally's vacation starts on March 28, how many days does she have to wait?

612.	A festival is celebrated on December 25 every year. If today is October 10, how many days are there until the festival?
613.	Maria's exam is scheduled for April 14. If today is April 1, how many days are there until her exam?
614.	Liam is counting down to New Year's Day. If today is December 15, how many days are left in the year?
615.	Jason is 3 years old. How many months old is he?
616.	Sarah has a 5-year membership at a library. How many months will her membership last?
617.	Alex worked at a company for 7 years before he retired. How many months did he work there?
618.	A warranty on a laptop lasts 2 years. How many months is this?
619.	Emily has been learning dance for 4 years. How many months has she been learning?
620.	A project takes 8 weeks to complete. Approximately how many months is this?

621.	If each semester is 16 weeks long, how many months is each semester?
622.	A summer camp lasts 6 weeks. How many months does the camp last?
623.	Lily's vacation lasted 12 weeks. How many months did she spend on vacation?
624.	Jake attended a training program for 10 weeks. Approximately how many months is that?
625.	Daniel has been practicing piano for 48 months. How many years is that?
626.	Anusha's job contract is for 60 months. How many years will she be working there?
627.	A car lease is for 36 months. How many years is the lease?
628.	If a child is 72 months old, how old is he in years?
629.	A training course lasts 24 months. How many years is this?
630.	If today is June 14 and Mia's exam is in 20 days, on what date will her exam be?
631.	Emma's holiday starts on July 1 and lasts for 45 days. On what date will her holiday end?

632.	If today is August 10 and Henry's birthday is in 15 days, what is Henry's birthday?
633.	A project started on March 1 and lasted 100 days. On what date did the project end?
634.	Leo's library book is due in 3 weeks. If today is October 4, on what date is the book due?
635.	If Maria's flight is on September 25 and today is September 5, how many days until her flight?
636.	A project deadline is on December 30. If today is December 1, how many days are left until the deadline?
637.	Jake's vacation starts on July 10, and today is June 25. How many days until his vacation?
638.	A report is due on February 20, but today is February 1. How many days are left?
639.	Sophia has a test on November 15, and today is November 1. How many days does she have to study?
640.	Each school term lasts 4 months. If there are 3 terms in a year, how many months are spent in school each year?

641.	An athlete trains 6 days a week. How many days does he train in 4 weeks?
642.	A worker takes 2 days off every month. How many days off will she take in a year?
643.	Jane volunteers every weekend (2 days). How many days does she volunteer in 6 months?
644.	If a plant takes 3 months to grow fully and is planted four times in a year, how many months are spent growing the plant each year?
645.	A 96-month contract needs to be divided into equal parts for 4 employees. How many months does each employee get?
646.	A gym membership of 24 months is split into 4 equal payment periods. How many months is each payment period?
647.	If a 120-month loan is divided into 10 equal parts, how many months is each part?
648.	Sarah's company plans a 48-week project and divides it equally among 4 teams. How many weeks will each team work?
649.	A 72-month study program is divided into 6 equal semesters. How many months does each semester last?

650.	Lisa's holiday is 3 weeks and 4 days long. If her holiday starts on July 10, on what date will it end?
651.	A movie marathon lasts 2 days and 6 hours. If it starts at 3:00 PM on June 5, at what time and date will it end?
652.	A summer camp lasts for 45 days and starts on July 1. On what date will the camp end?
653.	A scientist observes a planet every 6 days. If she starts on January 5, on what date will she make her 5th observation?
654.	A monthly bill of $30 is paid every 4 weeks. How much will be paid over 1 year?
655.	Emma's subscription is billed every 3 months at $50 per billing. How much will she pay in 2 years?
656.	If it takes 2 hours and 45 minutes to bake 3 batches of cookies, how long does it take to bake each batch?
657.	Sam is traveling for 3 weeks. He spends an average of $40 per day. How much does he spend in total?

658.	A factory runs 5 days a week, producing 100 units daily. How many units does it produce in 4 weeks?
659.	Lily's workout plan is 4 days per week for 30 minutes each day. How many hours does she work out in 3 months?
660.	Ryan has 3/4 of a pizza, and Amy has 5/6 of a pizza. Are these fractions proper or improper?
661.	Out of a full chocolate bar, Mike ate 8/7. What type of fraction is 8/7?
662.	Lily cut a ribbon into 9 parts, and each piece is 1/9 of the whole. What type of fraction is 1/9 ?
663.	If Bella ate 11/8 of a pie, is 11/8 a proper, improper, or mixed fraction?
664.	Adam split his time between two activities, spending 4/5 of an hour on reading and 9/5 of an hour on writing. Which fraction is improper?
665.	Identify whether 7/9, 8/3, and 5/7 are proper or improper fractions.
666.	Hannah read 13/12 of her book over the weekend. What type of fraction is this?

667.	David has 3/4 of a pencil left. Is this fraction proper or improper?
668.	Maya ate 5/4 of a cake and gave 1/4 to her friend. Which fraction is improper?
669.	Identify if 10/11, 15/10, and 6/5 are proper or improper.
670.	Arrange the fractions 1/3, 2/5, and 3/4 in ascending order.
671.	Sort the fractions 5/8, 2/3, and 3/5 from smallest to largest.
672.	Place these fractions in ascending order: 4/9 , 7/12, and 1/2.
673.	Which order should 3/7, 2/5, and 5/8 be in from least to greatest?
674.	Arrange 1/6, 3/8, and 7/12 in ascending order.
675.	Sort these fractions: 9/10, 3/4, and 5/6, starting with the smallest.
676.	Which comes first when ordered: 7/8, 5/6, or 3/4?
677.	Arrange 2/9, 5/7, and 4/6 from smallest to largest.

678.	Place the fractions 1/2, 5/8, and 7/10 in ascending order.
679.	Put 3/5, 1/4, and 2/3 in order from least to greatest.
680.	Arrange 5/6, 3/4, and 2/3 in descending order.
681.	Sort these fractions from greatest to smallest: 7/9, 5/8, and 3/4.
682.	Put 4/7, 6/10, and 1/2 in descending order.
683.	Arrange in descending order: 5/9, 2/3, and 4/5.
684.	Which fraction should come first in descending order: 3/4, 7/10, or 1/2?
685.	Place 2/5, 5/6, and 3/7 in descending order.
686.	Sort from largest to smallest: 3/8, 7/12, and 1/3 .
687.	Arrange 3/10, 5/9, and 2/3 in descending order.
688.	Put these in descending order: 6/7, 4/5, and 3/8.
689.	Place the fractions 7/10, 1/4 and 3/5 in descending order.
690.	Add 3/5 and 1/5.

691.	What is 2/3+1/6 ?
692.	Sum up 5/7and 3/7.
693.	Add 1/4, 1/2, and 1/8.
694.	Find the sum of 3/8 and 5/8.
695.	What is the total of 2/5 and 3/10?
696.	Add 3/4and 5/6.
697.	Find the sum of 7/9 and 4/9
698.	Add 1/6 and 5/12.
699.	What is 3/10+2/5?
700.	Subtract 1/6 from 5/6.
701.	What is 7/8 − 3/8?
702.	Find the result of 9/10−1/5109−51.
703.	Subtract 2/7from 5/7.
704.	What is 4/5−1/3?
705.	Subtract 1/4 from 7/8.
706.	Find 11/12−5/6.
707.	What is 3/5−1/10?
708.	Subtract 1/3 from 3/4.

709.	Find the difference of 7/8–1/4.
710.	Convert 11/4 to a mixed fraction.
711.	Write 17/5 as a mixed fraction.
712.	Express 9/2 as a mixed number.
713.	Change 13/3 into a mixed fraction.
714.	Convert 25/7 to a mixed fraction.
715.	Write 19/6 as a mixed number.
716.	Turn 15/4 into a mixed fraction.
717.	Change 22/5 into a mixed fraction.
718.	Convert 16/3 to a mixed number.
719.	Write 28/9 as a mixed fraction.
720.	Each term in the sequence 3, 12, 48, 192, ___ is multiplied by the same number. What is the missing term?
721.	What comes next in this series: 21, 32, 43, 54, ___?
722.	If a pattern starts with 7 and each next number increases by 4, what is the 10th term?
723.	In the sequence 1, 1, 2, 3, 5, 8, ___, what is the next number?

724.	Find the missing term: 64, 32, 16, 8, ___, 2.
725.	The pattern is 3, 7, 15, 31, ___, 127. What is the missing term?
726.	In the sequence 9, 18, 27, 36, ___, 54, which term is missing?
727.	If the pattern is 5, 11, 17, 23, ___, what is the 8th term?
728.	Find the next number in this pattern: 50, 45, 40, 35, ___.
729.	The series is 6, 10, 18, 34, 66, ___. What comes next?
730.	If a sequence begins with 12 and adds 6 each time, what is the 7th term?
731.	The pattern is 100, 85, 70, 55, ___, 25. What is the missing term?
732.	Find the next number: 13, 26, 24, 48, 46, ___.
733.	In a pattern, each number is obtained by subtracting 7 from the previous one. Starting from 70, what is the 6th term?
734.	The pattern is 1, 2, 4, 7, 11, ___, 22. What is the missing term?

735.	If each term in the sequence decreases by 9, starting at 63, what is the 5th term?
736.	The sequence is 12, 25, 23, 36, 34, ___, 47. What number is missing?
737.	Starting with 90 and subtracting 12 each time, what will the 8th term be?
738.	A sequence starts at 3 and each term is multiplied by 4. What is the 6th term?
739.	In the sequence 1024, 512, 256, ___, 64, 32, what number is missing?
740.	Each number in the pattern 2, 10, 50, 250, ___ is multiplied by the same factor. Find the missing term.
741.	In the sequence 81, 27, 9, ___, 1, what is the missing term?
742.	If the pattern starts at 5 and each term is multiplied by 5, what is the 5th term?
743.	A pattern of squares has 1 square in the first row, 3 in the second, 5 in the third, and 7 in the fourth. How many squares will be in the 6th row?

744.	A triangle pattern has 2 dots in the first row, 4 in the second, 6 in the third, and so on. How many dots will be in the 9th row?
745.	If a pattern of circles is arranged with 3 in the first row, 6 in the second, 9 in the third, what is the total number of circles after 7 rows?
746.	A row of hexagons starts with 1 hexagon, then 4 in the next row, and 9 in the next. If this pattern continues, how many hexagons are in the 5th row?
747.	A bus arrives at a stop every 12 minutes. If the first bus arrives at 8:15 AM, when will the 5th bus arrive?
748.	On the first day of a competition, a player scores 10 points. Each day, they score twice the previous day's points. How many points will they score on the 6th day?
749.	A plant grows 2 cm on the first day, 4 cm on the second, 6 cm on the third, and so on. How tall will it be after 7 days?
750.	A pattern of tiles has 4 tiles in the first row, 8 in the second, 12 in the third. How many tiles are there in the 10th row?

BREAK ZONE

751.	If yesterday was Monday, what day of the week will it be tomorrow?
752.	A rectangle can also be a square. (True/False)
753.	If you count from 1 to 50, how many times do you write the digit "5"?
754.	Two numbers add up to 12, and one number is 4 more than the other. What are the numbers?
755.	If a rooster lays an egg on top of a roof, which way will it roll?
756.	An isosceles triangle has two sides of equal length. (True/False)
757.	If you have keys for a car, a house, and a bike, and you use one key every day of the week, but only one key is used twice, which key is used twice?
758.	What comes next in the sequence: J, F, M, A, ___?
759.	What has hands but can't clap?

760.	If you are in third place in a race and pass the person in second place, what place are you in now?
761.	If all squares are rectangles, are all rectangles squares? (Yes/No)
762.	A triangle can have two right angles. (True/False)
763.	I have 3 keys: one for my locker, one for my bike, and one for my house. I use one key each day, but only one is used twice. Which key is used twice?
764.	What comes next in the sequence: 5, 10, 20, 40, ___?
765.	What is full of holes but can still hold water?
766.	If you have a basket with 3 apples and you take away 2, how many do you have?
767.	If you move from January to February, how many months are you moving?
768.	The sum of two odd numbers is always even. (True/False)
769.	A farmer has 17 sheep and all but 9 die. How many are left?

770.	What comes next in the sequence: 1, 1, 2, 3, 5, 8, ___?
771.	If Tuesday is three days before Friday, what day is two days after Tuesday?
772.	The perimeter of a shape is always greater than its area. (True/False)
773.	If you count from 1 to 100, how many times do you write the digit "7"?
774.	I have keys for a car, a bike, and a drawer. I use one key every day of the week, but only one key is used twice. Which key is used twice?
775.	What comes next in the sequence: A, E, I, O, ___?
776.	What has a neck but no head?
777.	Jack measured a rope and found it to be 5.7 meters long. He then cut off 125 cm from it. What is the length of the remaining rope in meters?
778.	Emma has a ribbon that is 3 meters long. She cuts it into pieces, each 40 cm in length. How many full pieces can she cut, and what length of ribbon will remain?
779.	A garden is 2.5 kilometers in length. A pathway covering half of this distance is built

	along one side of the garden. How many meters long is the pathway?
780.	Lily walks 600 meters to school every day. How many kilometers does she walk to and from school in one week (5 school days)?
781.	Tom measured the height of his plant each month. In January, it was 75 cm tall, and by June, it had grown to 1.2 meters. How many centimeters did the plant grow from January to June?
782.	If you are fourth in a line and the person behind you is third, what position are you in?
783.	If April 1st is a Tuesday, what day is April 30th?
784.	A parallelogram has two pairs of parallel sides. (True/False)
785.	If you have 2 apples and eat one, how many do you have left?
786.	A fence is built along the perimeter of a rectangular field that is 120 meters long and 80 meters wide. If each meter of fencing costs $5, what is the total cost of the fencing?
787.	A train track is 1.75 kilometers long. If it is divided into sections of 250 meters each, how

	many full sections are there, and what length of track will be left unsectioned?
788.	A car traveled 150 kilometers in one direction and returned by the same route. If the trip took 3 hours in total, what was the car's average speed in meters per second?
789.	A swimmer practices in a 25-meter pool. If she swims 60 laps each day, how many kilometers does she swim in one week (7 days)?
790.	A construction company needs 24 kilometers of metal wire. They already have 14,500 meters of wire. How many more meters do they need to reach their goal?
791.	If 5x + 3 = 18, what is the value of x?
792.	What is 1/3 of 1/2 of 1/6 of 72?
793.	The ratio of boys to girls in a class is 2:3. If there are 10 boys, how many girls are there?
794.	What two numbers multiply to 30 and add up to 13?
795.	A jar contains twice as many red marbles as blue marbles. If there are 18 marbles in total, how many red marbles are there?

796.	Find the missing number in the pattern: 3, 9, 15, 21, ___.
797.	A train travels at 60 km/h. How far will it travel in 2.5 hours?
798.	What is the sum of all the digits from 1 to 9?
799.	If 6 spiders have 48 legs, how many legs do 9 spiders have?
800.	How many odd numbers are there between 1 and 101?
801.	If $4y - 5 = 15$, what is the value of y?
802.	What is 1/4 of 1/3 of 1/2 of 48?
803.	The ratio of cats to dogs is 4:5. If there are 16 cats, how many dogs are there?
804.	What two numbers multiply to 24 and add up to 10?
805.	A basket contains twice as many oranges as apples. If there are 20 fruits in total, how many oranges are there?
806.	A watermelon weighs 3.75 kg. After slicing, 500 grams of the watermelon is eaten. What is the weight of the remaining watermelon in kilograms?

807.	An empty box weighs 800 grams. When filled with books, the total weight is 4.5 kg. How much do the books alone weigh in grams?
808.	A chef has 2 kg of flour. He uses 250 grams to bake bread and 750 grams to make a cake. How many grams of flour are left?
809.	A shipment of apples weighs 35 kg. Each apple weighs about 250 grams. Approximately how many apples are in the shipment?
810.	A sack of rice weighs 20 kg. If 1 kg of rice is used each day, how many days will it take to use up 75% of the sack's weight?
811.	A container holds 12.5 kg of sand. If 2.75 kg is removed, how many grams of sand remain in the container?
812.	Find the missing number in the pattern: 5, 10, 20, 35, ____.
813.	A car travels at 80 km/h. How far will it travel in 3.5 hours?
814.	What is the sum of all the digits from 1 to 10?
815.	If 7 spiders have 56 legs, how many legs do 10 spiders have?

816.	How many even numbers are there between 1 and 101?
817.	If 2z + 8 = 20, what is the value of z?
818.	What is 1/2 of 1/4 of 1/5 of 40?
819.	The ratio of apples to oranges is 5:7. If there are 25 apples, how many oranges are there?
820.	John has a sack of potatoes weighing 5.2 kg. He splits the sack into bags, each weighing 650 grams. How many full bags can he make, and what weight of potatoes will remain?
821.	A farmer has two boxes of oranges. One box weighs 4,500 grams, and the other weighs 6.75 kg. What is the total weight of both boxes in kilograms?
822.	A truck carries 1.5 tons of cement to a construction site. If each bag of cement weighs 50 kg, how many bags are on the truck?
823.	A goldsmith melts down two gold bars weighing 850 grams and 1.2 kg. He then uses 750 grams of this gold to make jewellery. What is the weight of the remaining gold in grams?
824.	What two numbers multiply to 18 and add up to 9?

825.	A box contains twice as many blue balls as red balls. If there are 22 balls in total, how many blue balls are there?
826.	Find the missing number in the pattern: 4, 12, 20, 28, ___.
827.	A cyclist travels at 12 km/h. How far will they travel in 4 hours?
828.	What is the sum of all the digits from 1 to 11?
829.	If 8 spiders have 64 legs, how many legs do 12 spiders have?
830.	How many odd numbers are there between 1 and 111?
831.	If $3x + 7 = 25$, what is the value of x?
832.	What is 1/5 of 1/3 of 1/2 of 60?
833.	The ratio of girls to boys is 3:4. If there are 12 girls, how many boys are there?
834.	What two numbers multiply to 16 and add up to 10?
835.	A container holds twice as many pencils as pens. If there are 30 items in total, how many pencils are there?

836.	A large tank can hold 25 liters of water. If 3,750 milliliters are removed from the tank, how much water remains in liters?
837.	A jar contains 3.25 liters of honey. If Lily uses 450 milliliters of honey to make desserts, how many milliliters of honey are left in the jar?
838.	Emma has a juice container that holds 1.5 liters. She pours the juice equally into 6 cups. How many milliliters of juice are in each cup?
839.	A tank holds 18,000 milliliters of water. How many 2-liter bottles can be filled from the tank, and what amount of water, in milliliters, will be left over?
840.	A swimming pool holds 2,000 liters of water. If the pool loses 120 liters of water each day due to evaporation, how much water will be left after 5 days?
841.	Find the missing number in the pattern: 6, 15, 24, 33, ___.
842.	A boat travels at 20 km/h. How far will it travel in 3 hours?
843.	A rectangular box has a length of 20 cm, a width of 10 cm, and a height of 15 cm. What is the volume of the box in cubic centimeters

	(cm³), and how many liters is this equivalent to?
844.	A medicine bottle contains 0.5 liters of liquid. If each dose is 25 milliliters, how many doses can be given from the entire bottle?
845.	A juice factory produces 45 liters of juice every hour. How many milliliters of juice does the factory produce in 3.5 hours?
846.	A fish tank has a capacity of 120 liters. Due to leakage, the tank loses 15 milliliters every minute. If it starts full, how much water, in liters, will remain after 2 hours?
847.	A bottle holds 2.4 liters of water. If a family drinks 750 milliliters every day, how many days will it take them to finish 3 full bottles of water?
848.	What is the sum of all the digits from 1 to 12?
849.	If 9 spiders have 72 legs, how many legs do 15 spiders have?
850.	How many even numbers are there between 1 and 111?
851.	If $4x - 9 = 11$, what is the value of x?
852.	What is 1/6 of 1/3 of 1/2 of 36?

853.	The ratio of cats to dogs is 2:3. If there are 14 cats, how many dogs are there?
854.	What two numbers multiply to 20 and add up to 12?
855.	A shelf contains twice as many fiction books as non-fiction books. If there are 18 books in total, how many fiction books are there?
856.	Find the missing number in the pattern: 7, 21, 35, 49, ___.
857.	A plane travels at 500 km/h. How far will it travel in 2 hours?
858.	If 10 spiders have 80 legs, how many legs do 18 spiders have?
859.	How many odd numbers are there between 1 and 121?
860.	If $5y + 6 = 31$, what is the value of y?
861.	What is 1/7 of 1/3 of 1/5 of 70?
862.	The ratio of apples to bananas is 3:5. If there are 21 apples, how many bananas are there?
863.	What two numbers multiply to 25 and add up to 16?

864.	A drawer holds twice as many socks as gloves. If there are 24 items in total, how many socks are there?
865.	Find the missing number in the pattern: 8, 24, 40, 56, ___.
866.	A train travels at 100 km/h. How far will it travel in 2.5 hours?
867.	What is the sum of all the digits from 1 to 14?
868.	If 11 spiders have 88 legs, how many legs do 20 spiders have?
869.	How many even numbers are there between 1 and 121?
870.	If 6x - 4 = 32, what is the value of x?
871.	What is 1/8 of 1/4 of 1/3 of 96?
872.	The ratio of girls to boys is 5:6. If there are 20 girls, how many boys are there?
873.	What two numbers multiply to 28 and add up to 17?
874.	A cabinet contains twice as many cups as plates. If there are 26 items in total, how many cups are there?

875.	Find the missing number in the pattern: 9, 27, 45, 63, ___.
876.	A car travels at 70 km/h. How far will it travel in 4 hours?
877.	What is the sum of all the digits from 1 to 15?
878.	If 12 spiders have 96 legs, how many legs do 25 spiders have?
879.	How many odd numbers are there between 1 and 131?
880.	If $7y + 5 = 47$, what is the value of y?
881.	What is 1/9 of 1/4 of 1/3 of 81?
882.	The ratio of apples to oranges is 4:5. If there are 32 apples, how many oranges are there?
883.	What two numbers multiply to 30 and add up to 19?
884.	A basket holds twice as many strawberries as blueberries. If there are 22 berries in total, how many strawberries are there?
885.	Find the missing number in the pattern: 10, 30, 50, 70, ___.
886.	A cyclist travels at 15 km/h. How far will they travel in 5 hours?

887.	What is the sum of all the digits from 1 to 16?
888.	If 13 spiders have 104 legs, how many legs do 30 spiders have?
889.	How many even numbers are there between 1 and 131?
890.	If 8x - 7 = 49, what is the value of x?
891.	What is 1/10 of 1/5 of 1/2 of 100?
892.	The ratio of cats to dogs is 3:4. If there are 21 cats, how many dogs are there?
893.	What two numbers multiply to 35 and add up to 18?
894.	A jar contains twice as many green marbles as red marbles. If there are 18 marbles in total, how many green marbles are there?
895.	Find the missing number in the pattern: 11, 33, 55, 77, ____.
896.	A boat travels at 25 km/h. How far will it travel in 6 hours?
897.	What is the sum of all the digits from 1 to 17?
898.	If 14 spiders have 112 legs, how many legs do 35 spiders have?

899.	How many odd numbers are there between 1 and 141?
900.	If 9y + 6 = 54, what is the value of y?
901.	What is 1/11 of 1/6 of 1/3 of 99?
902.	The ratio of apples to bananas is 5:7. If there are 35 apples, how many bananas are there?
903.	What two numbers multiply to 40 and add up to 22?
904.	A box contains twice as many pens as pencils. If there are 24 items in total, how many pens are there?
905.	Find the missing number in the pattern: 12, 36, 60, 84, ___.
906.	A plane travels at 600 km/h. How far will it travel in 1.5 hours?
907.	What is the sum of all the digits from 1 to 18?
908.	If 15 spiders have 120 legs, how many legs do 40 spiders have?
909.	How many even numbers are there between 1 and 141?
910.	If 10x - 8 = 72, what is the value of x?
911.	What is 1/12 of 1/5 of 1/4 of 120?

912.	The ratio of girls to boys is 4:5. If there are 16 girls, how many boys are there?
913.	What two numbers multiply to 45 and add up to 26?
914.	A shelf contains twice as many fiction books as non-fiction books. If there are 20 books in total, how many fiction books are there?
915.	Find the missing number in the pattern: 13, 39, 65, 91, ___.
916.	A train travels at 90 km/h. How far will it travel in 4.5 hours?
917.	What is the sum of all the digits from 1 to 19?
918.	If 16 spiders have 128 legs, how many legs do 50 spiders have?
919.	How many odd numbers are there between 1 and 151?
920.	What is the perimeter of a square with side length 6 units?
921.	What is the area of a rectangle with a length of 8 units and a width of 3 units?
922.	What is the volume of a cube with a side length of 4 units?

923.	How many faces does a cube have?
924.	A triangle has angles of 60°, 60°, and __°. What is the missing angle?
925.	What is the perimeter of a triangle with sides of 5, 7, and 9 units?
926.	How many lines of symmetry does a square have?
927.	A pattern of circles has 1 circle in the first row, 4 in the second row, and 9 in the third row. How many circles are in the fourth row?
928.	How many edges does a rectangular prism have?
929.	What is the angle between the hour and minute hands at 4:00?
930.	How many small cubes with side length 2 units can fit in a larger cube with side length 8 units?
931.	If a rope is cut into 5 equal pieces and each piece is 6 cm long, how long was the original rope?
932.	How many vertices does a pentagon have?
933.	What comes next in the pattern: triangle, square, pentagon, hexagon, ___?

934.	How many sides does a decagon have?
935.	What is the area of a square with a perimeter of 16 units?
936.	How many lines of symmetry does an equilateral triangle have?
937.	If a hexagon is divided into triangles by connecting every vertex to the centre, how many triangles are formed?
938.	A tank has a length of 10 cm, a width of 5 cm, and a height of 4 cm. What is its volume in cubic centimeters?
939.	A quadrilateral has three angles measuring 90°, 80°, and 95°. What is the measure of the fourth angle?
940.	A number is multiplied by 4, then 6 is subtracted from the result, giving 26. What is the original number?
941.	A number is multiplied by 5 and then divided by 10. If the result is 15, what was the original number?
942.	Two numbers have a sum of 50 and a difference of 14. What are the two numbers?
943.	A and B start from the same point and walk in opposite directions. After walking 5 km each,

	they turn around and walk back 2 km. How far apart are they now?
944.	The sum of three consecutive odd numbers is 75. What are these numbers?
945.	If 3 more than twice a certain number is equal to 21, what is the number?
946.	When a certain number is divided by 5, the remainder is 3. What could be the smallest value of this number greater than 100?
947.	The sum of the ages of two people is 45. In 5 years, one of them will be twice as old as the other. How old are they?
948.	In a three-digit number, the hundreds digit is twice the tens digit, and the tens digit is twice the units digit. If the sum of the digits is 14, what is the number?
949.	A farmer plants rows of trees. In each row, the number of trees is double the number in the previous row. If the first row has 3 trees, how many trees will the 6th row have?
950.	The perimeter of a square is equal to the perimeter of a rectangle with length 8 cm and width 6 cm. What is the side length of the square?

951.	A rectangular garden is 12 meters long and 9 meters wide. If a pathway 1 meter wide is added around the garden, what is the total area of the pathway?
952.	The area of a rectangle is 96 square cm, and its length is twice its width. What are the dimensions of the rectangle?
953.	A square and a rectangle have the same perimeter. If the side length of the square is 12 cm, and the length of the rectangle is 18 cm, what is its width?
954.	A pattern goes as follows: 5, 11, 17, 23, ___. What will be the 10th term in the pattern?
955.	What is the 7th term in the sequence where each term is the previous term multiplied by 3, starting with 2?
956.	If each term in a sequence increases by 6, starting with 5, what is the 15th term?
957.	A number pattern starts with 7 and each term is 4 more than the previous term. What is the 12th term?
958.	Each term in a sequence is the sum of the two previous terms, starting with 3 and 5. What is the 6th term?

959.	In the sequence 3, 9, 27, ___, 243, what number is missing?
960.	Place the numbers 1 to 6 in the circles of a triangle so that each side of the triangle adds up to the same total. (Hint: each side should add up to 9.)
961.	I am a two-digit number. The sum of my digits is 12, and the difference between my digits is 4. What number am I?
962.	If a number is doubled and then increased by 10, the result is 50. What is the number?
963.	If today is Wednesday, what day of the week will it be 100 days from now?
964.	A farmer has chickens and cows. Altogether, they have 36 heads and 100 legs. How many chickens and how many cows are there?
965.	Fill in the blanks: 7 + __ + 5 = 20 - __. Both blanks must have the same number. What is the number?
966.	What is the sum of all the digits from 1 to 13?
967.	Find a two-digit number that, when multiplied by 4, gives a product that reads the same forward and backward (a palindrome).

968.	You have 21 cupcakes. You want to distribute them equally among a group of people such that each person gets an odd number of cupcakes. What is the maximum number of people you can have in the group?
969.	If you swap the digits of a two-digit number, you get a new number that is 27 less than the original number. What is the original number?
970.	A book has a total of 300 pages. If you start reading on page 56 and read every 5th page, what will be the last page you read that is less than or equal to 300?
971.	Identify the number that does not belong in this sequence: 2, 4, 8, 10, 16, 20, 32.
972.	In 5 years, a father will be twice as old as his son. Currently, the father is 40 years old. How old is the son now?
973.	If APPLE is coded as 51135, and ORANGE is coded as 153751, what would BANANA be coded as?
974.	Find the missing number in this sequence: 3, 8, 15, 24, __, 48.
975.	Two trains are on the same track, 400 km apart. They are moving towards each other,

	each at a speed of 80 km/h. How long will it take before they meet?
976.	A bucket is half-full. If you add 4 liters, it becomes three-quarters full. What is the total capacity of the bucket?
977.	A shopkeeper buys a watch for $150 and sells it for $180. What is the percentage profit?
978.	I am a two-digit number. My tens digit is twice my units digit, and the sum of my digits is 12. What is my number?
979.	You have 20 dominoes. If each domino weighs 35 grams, and the total weight of all dominoes is 750 grams, how many dominoes are missing?
980.	A painter can paint a wall in 4 hours. If he paints 3 walls in one day, taking a 1-hour break between each wall, how many hours does he spend painting in a day?
981.	A monkey climbs a banana tree that is 10 meters tall. Each day, it climbs up 3 meters but slides down 2 meters at night. How many days will it take for the monkey to reach the top?
982.	A chocolate bar costs $3. If you get a free chocolate bar for every 3 wrappers returned,

	how many chocolates can you get if you start with $18?
983.	A pattern of shapes follows this order: Triangle, Square, Circle, Triangle, Square, Circle. What shape will be the 15th shape in the sequence?
984.	When a number is reversed and added to itself, the result is 121. What is the number?
985.	You have 9 identical-looking balls, but one is slightly heavier than the others. Using only a balance scale and two weighing, how can you find the heavier ball?
986.	At what time between 1:00 and 2:00 will the hour and minute hands of a clock overlap?
987.	If you roll two six-sided dice, what is the probability of rolling a sum of 7?
988.	A brick weighs one kilogram plus half of its own weight. How much does the brick weigh?
989.	Four friends need to cross a narrow bridge at night with only one flashlight. They can only cross two at a time, and they each take different times to cross: 1 minute, 2 minutes, 7 minutes, and 10 minutes. What is the minimum

	total time required for all four friends to cross the bridge?
990.	I have no sides. People often use me to represent nothing. Who am I?
991.	I am an even number. I am greater than 10 but less than 20. The sum of my digits is 8. Who am I?
992.	I am a number. If you multiply me by 5 and then subtract 3, the result is 17. Who am I?
993.	I am a type of number. I can be divided by exactly two different numbers: 1 and myself. I am greater than 10 but less than 20. Who am I?
994.	I am a three-digit number. My tens and hundreds digits are the same, and my units digit is zero. I am a multiple of 11. Who am I?
995.	I am a shape with three sides. People often use me to represent strength and stability. Who am I?
996.	I am the smallest number that is a multiple of both 4 and 6. Who am I?
997.	I am a 2D shape. I have four equal sides, and all my angles are right angles. You often see me on a chessboard. Who am I?

998.	I am a number that doesn't change no matter how many times you multiply me by myself. I am the answer to any number raised to the power of zero. Who am I?
999.	I am a number that is the sum of two consecutive numbers, and I am greater than 10 but less than 20. My tens digit is twice my unis digit. Who am I?
1000.	I am less than 50 and a multiple of both 6 and 9. I am also an even number. Who am I?

www.ingramcontent.com/pod-product-compliance
Lightning Source LLC
Chambersburg PA
CBHW021553150726
47990CB00006B/2523